THE
TIMELESS

By Nathan D. Godolphin

The Timeless

Published by Spirit Scribe.
www.spiritscribe.co.uk

First published 2017.

ISBN 978-1-911594-03-1.

IT'S ALL HAPPENING NOW!

PRESENTING IT ALL
IN LINEAR TIME AND SPACE...

THE TOTALITY- AND THE REALITY-

OF HERENOW.

THE NOWNESS
OF OUR BEING HERE.

THE NOWNESS OF
OUR BEING

LOVE!

This is my Primary offering to the world. All my work revolves around this central understanding. It is a unique 'Way of Seeing' that I consider to be THE Yoga Philosophy. And yet I don't think it's been presented quite like this before.

This Truth is Timeless and Eternal... touched upon by all the Great Mystery traditions.

Truth is Timeless and Eternal- and yet it operates in time and space.

And this Simple and Profound synthesis is new.

This model is necessary in these times. It re-establishes meaning in our lives, without antiquated scripture and old techniques.

It is Consciousness's 'Way of Seeing'. Diversity, happening in You. And you, happening in the Wholeness of One.

If that sounds confusing, read on. All becomes clear.

It is no less than the Meaning of Life we all seek... And the Existence that is Ours (Already).

This Love Being Here.

An understanding of the Universal 'Divine Architecture' presented in this book brings meaning and value to the parts we play, and the spaces we inhabit in this world of ours- which is none other than the crystallisation of Spirit.

Spirit is what it's all about.

Self-Realisation leads us to this Understanding.

That there is just one thing going on- it is Perfect Peace, it is HereNow... And WE ARE IT.

And you find this Truth through asking the question, of yourself... WHO AM I?

THIS IS HOW I CAME TO THIS.

THIS IS HOW OUR CONSCIOUSNESS

RETURNS HOME

...AND LIVES OUT AGAIN IN LOVE.

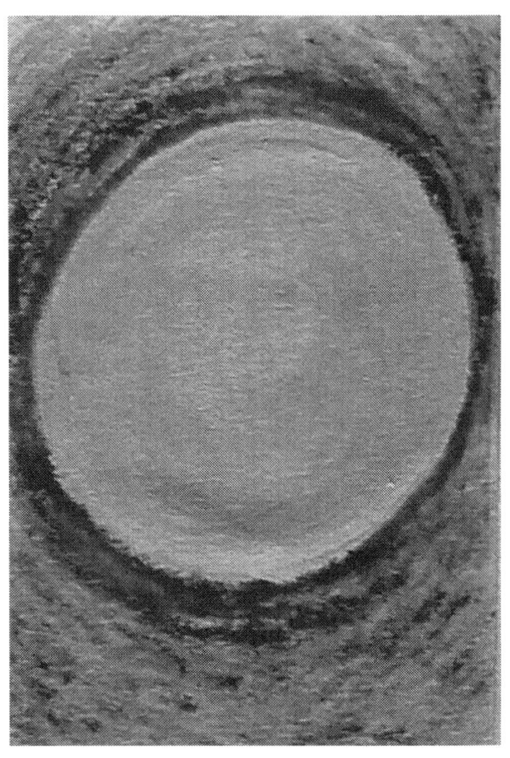

Oneness is All There Is.
We came from One.
The Timeless Essence Being That We Are.

This is Consciousness/God/Love/Life Itself!

It is Whole. Complete. Everything and All. Totality.

It contains everything, yet without being differentiated.

It is Undifferentiated Being!

(For if it was differentiated, it wouldn't be One! It would be many!

And it's not many... Is it? Do read on...)...

The One Singularity.

The Indescribable Beauty-One That Exists 'prior' to Creation.
'Before' manifestation. Before time and space are even born.

'Before' Essence springs forth into experience-
into all the things and stuff of life.

Before the trees, the plants, the animals; the birds, the wind, the rain...

This Oneness is Everything and Nothing.

Unmanifest. Pure Being. Pure Potential.

*

But it lacks something.

The one thing Oneness does not have is experience.

It lacks its own expression.

For how can Oneness express Oneness? It is only One.
To what or to whom 'else' would it express?

It can't *do* anything. It can only Be.

Itself.

*

Perfection, yes...

but nothing else.

For it is Pure Being.

There is no 'other' in its realm!

It is Its own realm of Silence, Peace and Love. Pure Bliss!

And it wants to know Itself. To express and experience Itself! It wants to know Its Bliss.

It wants to know Its Perfection.

To see Its Majesty!

To express Its Mystery!

The Great Mystery of Life!

*

And so there was- and is- this desire for Oneness to be something other than Oneness.

To create a manifest version/vision-
or versions/visions-
of Itself.

Some(times) in line with Bliss,
some(times) not.
Either way...

To be in experience.

*

Which means Oneness splitting into two... and more... and many, and more and more...

For in order to have experience we need separation.

That's just the way it is.

The Seer and the seen;

The Knower and the known;

The Experiencer and the experience;

The Dreamer and the dream.

This is the duality... and the multiplicity.

The separation.

*

Separation does not exist in Oneness.
For Oneness is Always One.
Only. Always. One.

Remember?

*

And so Consciousness needs to 'step down' from Purity, from Unity...

...or appear to do so.

Consciousness needs to split...
or contract...

or somehow move away from Oneness...

give way to 'something else'...

remove itself from Oneness...

from Itself...

(or appear to do so)...

to somehow be balanced by shadow...

to introduce some aspect of make-believe, illusion...

...or the apparent absence of Itself... (When it can never really be absent because it is All That Is)...

To blow Itself apart, to fragment itself into pieces... like a mirror, broken...

...or a veil of separative perception obscuring its Original Nature.

To hold its Light in the balance of a dualistic world platform of both light and dark- as the One Pure Light Projector, shining its Light, appearing as scenes, when viewed through various filters.

In a Divine Matrix of possibility...

All for the sake of an experience...

This One Pure Consciousness allows.

The desire for experience builds and builds and builds... first a small urge- the impulse growing and growing and growing- until it can no longer be held... it cannot be held back anymore...

And with the desire to experience Itself, Oneness bursts out into experience. Pwaaaaaarrrrrrr!

The Big Bang... The beginning of the Universe... The birth of a Star... and stars.

This is The Dream of Our Creation!

Pure Consciousness, bursting apart into fragments of Itself.

Different levels and stratas and striations, and 'types' of consciousness.

Many plants, trees, animals, people, places, things, and possible combinations thereof, emerging in time. Vast spectrums of colour, of sound, of shape and size, forms and ways of Being.

This is both the birth of the Universe, and the birth of us. One and the same.

It is none other than *our* desire to experience *our*selves.

For the Truth is We Are This Whole.

It is our Self. Our Source.

Our Being.

*

The Creative Power of the Universe is the Divine Power from which we are not separate.

Being souls of the One Spirit.

We are a product of the Universe, are we not?

Oneness gave birth to time and space and star-stuff crystallised in and on the Earth.

From the climactic explosion of Its Initial Desire, Oneness came to experience Itself!

Yes, Oneness gave birth to parts, to fragments, to different ways and forms.

It is giving birth now... as we are...

Why?

To Know Itself!

This is the Purpose of Creation!

All these possibilities of experience so we can learn who we are and what this life is all about.

God seeking to Know Itself. Consciousness seeking to know- or experience its knowing... of what it is.

What We Are!

It's all the same thing! The same Oneness. Because there is no other.

But we forget our Unity... our Oneness.

And for the very purpose of this experience.

For how can we have experience if we were still unmanifest Oneness?! If we still remembered?!

If we are still unmanifest Oneness, there are no parts to the play! No props! No characters!

*

So the veil must enter. Our perception of ourselves reduced to much less than we are.

Consciousness shrunk down.

Oneness is Beautiful... but it seeks to know that Beauty,
and this 'veil' the price to pay- the ticket for the ride!

Otherwise it would be no fun, for we would see it's all our own finger, pointing back to us. (And we will, eventually, see this...).

Consciousness has been given the opportunity to enter into the Dream of Itself.

To see it for Itself! To See Itself for Itself. First hand. Direct. This is what we are here for.

To have the Journey of that Seeing... not just 'As Is', but in obscurity and clarity. In duality. For as we have seen, that is the only way it can happen.

And we are the Seeing!

Nobody can see it for us.

We have to see for ourselves.

And we do see for ourselves.

*

Whatever it is we see- or *how* we see it- our world view- is a testament to our particular level, or condition, of Consciousness.

Whether we are operating from our particular configuration of consciousness in duality, seeing with our own personal filters and lenses based on our own personal accumulated time-space experience... or Seeing as the Pure Oneness We Are.

Seeing with Oneness is more a harmonising with 'What Is'- a resonance of Ultimate Being, whereas seeing with duality is like defining against a contrast of what isn't. What you are, brought into focus against what you are not. A relative way of seeing.

*

Sometimes there's a lot of stuff in our lives blocking clear seeing. Blocking the harmony of Being. Stuff that drives us on, but at some time we need to let go of. And when the time is right, we shed it like an old skin.

All our separative ambitions that we have to set us apart from others in Life... when Life is All we are, and all others are also.

We see the futility of trying to out-do Life. Of trying to break ourselves off from it to overcome it.

Yes, we have seen that to have experience we need duality.

Multiplicity. Separation gives us the possibility of different combinations, different configurations, facets and expressions of Being. Of that Original Being.

We appear to live in a world of plus and minus, up and down, left and right, here and there, me and you, this and that.

This is so that Consciousness can play!

And we explore this play, as we rightly should.

Consciousness dancing in and out of what it is.
To know what it is and what it isn't,
what it isn't and what it is.

The Non-Dual reaches
into the world of time.

The Non-Dual reaches
into the world of the dual. Manifestation of separate form.

This is Oneness extending Itself into a dream of 'not One'...

Peace seeking to find Itself, in a world of noise.

The Ultimate Truth, playing in the relative truths.

To See Itself. To be recognised. To be seen and heard... and to see and hear.

*

But we can get lost in this.

It's All One Being, masquerading as separate. It can be such a convincing show!

We might pretend we are separate too. Even if we don't know we are pretending.

Perhaps we believe it for real. We might really feel it. That we are separate. We probably do... to some extent.

Separation can feel very real. At least at times... and in certain spaces... the nooks and crannies of our own consciousness.

A strand- or a spark- of consciousness within a body... the whole tapestry of which we are a part, sometimes tragically obscured.

It can be very isolating. Hope may appear futile.

Isolated minds...

But by our own understanding!

Our own state of Being.

*

There is a time when it is necessary to reach back into the very Core of our Being... of Who We Are.

There comes a time when there is the urge to do so.

For the veil can be overcome. It can be lifted. We can see through the mists of time and space.

But only when we see beyond the constructs we have invented and lost ourselves in... which are the very walls of the separation we otherwise enforce. The walls of the world and the walls in our own minds.

This is our own process. We do it for our self. No other way.

What exclusory 'things' are we investing ourselves in? What are we excluding? Leaving outside our definition?

What are we aligned to? What are we identifying with?

The Wholeness or the part?

Oneness or separation?

*

As we head out on our Divine Journey, away from the Oneness we were born from, the very nature of the experience (being separate) can condition us into the belief that we are separate fragments. Physical mind-body units only. That that is who we are, and all there is to us.

Not so. But oh, the experience can be pervasive! Indeed, it *is* pervasive. It has to be. For if we stayed in conscious connection to our Source- with this Spiritual Awareness- we wouldn't have the experience of forgetting and then remembering again.

Forgetting and remembering- another facet of the duality. The whole fragmented process is fuelled by this duality of being. This is the mechanism. Turning.

For in Oneness, nothing happening. Only Pure Conscious Love!

Which is great.

But we want(ed) experience.

*

And so we have it!

Consciousness turns from Centre.

Out, out, out we go. Bye Mum, Bye Dad, see you later!

Out on our exploration.

Knowing it or not, it is the exploration of ourselves. And our Self.

For we are the world we are exploring, and everything is connected, on a deeper level than our separative perception might have us realise.

We play-act as different characters, thinking it's all real-
indeed, we are different characters in the dream- and it is real...
But it is just different aspects of the One Consciousness We Are.

And we are working and playing
through these different aspects,
to the One Divine Truth That We Are.

For this is the movement...

'Away from' to 'come back' to.

Away from to come back to,
with the Knowledge of the experience
(before we forget it again, and start over...).

And it's all happening at once, because it's all happening now.
(But we'll come to that later...).

*

So, we know now that Consciousness splits apart in order to experience Itself. We know at least as an idea, if not felt on a felt level. If you don't yet feel it on a felt level.

This experience we have happens in duality, and this experience is what duality is all about.

Duality is all about this experience.

For without duality, no experience!

Duality can be painful, it can be hard.

But it is the beautiful experience that has been afforded us.

Joy and Sadness are but the two sides of the same coin... and so close together when we see. One Currency of Love! True Value.

Such a narrow turning pinpoint of Presence- and vast in its outpour!

Out from One Point Centre, into separation...

Plus, minus, left and right, up and down, light and dark.

One Primordial Cosmic Light
splitting into light and dark.

The shadow enters as the balancer to the light
(all for the sake of experience...
or the appearance of experience).

Objects form, create a shadow-play of light. Light and shadows cast in separation.

All degrees and all spectrums and all possible combinations of experience.

And we go out into these fragments. We love it! All the possibilities to explore...

Further and further out we go... our Original Love, fuelling us on.

It's exciting! It's New! It's Fresh!

We're learning and growing... defining ourselves...

Oneness is exploring its own territory!

The playmat of time and space that is its own effulgence!

And it is an experience... and our knowledge is experiential. We only learn through experience, which modifies our understanding of the world and ourselves.

In time and space; the desired journey.

Whatever it is.

*

But it reaches the limits of its own experience.

It goes out far enough in its enjoyment and suffering in experience.

Its learning and playing that necessarily involves the forgetting of the Source.

(For with full remembrance, no experience).

It begins to lose steam.

We begin to lose steam.

To lose Heart.

Or the pace of it gathers and becomes too great! We're almost spinning out too far!

Where's our Centre anymore?

*

In going out so far, into expression, more and more combinations of experience, and finer and finer details, nuances and subtleties of being and categories of thought and analysis and boxes for it all (never mind the mind-numbing trinkets and flash-in-the-pan pleasure death loss!)... This Pure Being, apparently fragmented in time and space...

...has a crisis of meaning.

As we do.

*

Boxed up, lost. Duality can almost take us. Can almost blow us apart too far. Too much. Like we've defined ourselves into the ground. Excluded too much. Narrowed ourselves down to nothing of any Reality anymore. Weighed ourselves down with stuff.

We may have got lost in it. But we do not need to get- or rather we do not need to stay- lost in the dream, the noise, the separate. The details at the expense of The Whole.

Indeed, the crisis of the head may bring about a shift into the Spiritual Heart. The filtering of this knowledge into Reality. Feeding back into Core Consciousness. Direct.

It is not the Pure Being that has a crisis of meaning (for it is always Whole)... Pure Being Always 'Is'... but the aspect of it that has forgotten this Wholeness- that has forgotten that by itself, it is just an aspect- the unenlightened you and me. The human being that has pursued separation and almost lost itself.

It is the crisis of separation.

*

While finding out many things, Consciousness has forgotten Its Core Self.

We have forgotten ourselves. Our Core Self. (Same One).

And it's time to come back. (In all our different paths and ways).

Out of the illusion and back into the Real.

It is not the plan for us (for consciousness) to go out forever.

Love does not work like that. Not in this world. Not on this Earth. Unless something goes horribly wrong... which it won't... because it can't.

Circles and cycles are how Consciousness operates in this world. Seasons return, waves and tides go out to come back.

We go out to come back in. Not just to come back in. But to dream. To follow our dreams. To Journey. To reach the end point. And to return with the knowledge of ourselves... as we dissolve back in to Source.

Through This Divine Journey.

*

It's time to remember.
(We have forgotten long enough...)

The facade becomes too much.

We feel false.
Lacking. Missing.
What's the point?

The separate part- the crystallised and crystallising Source Energy, the aspect of The Original Consciousness that has gone so far out in its forgetting, its story-telling, web-weaving, world-creating, mischief-making, love-elating, conflict, competition, and rollercoaster riding...

So far out in its separation (for separation is necessary to experience! Remember this also!)... that it feels disconnected from meaning.

Disconnected from Life.

The Life That It Is!

Disconnected from Itself. From Life Itself.

Because it has forgotten Itself.

It has forgotten its Source.

The All-Knowing Higher Self of each individual.

Its Deeper Unity.

The Timeless Essence it was born from.

(All necessary... it would seem!).

*

We can't continue the way we have been going.

And the real change is not in a rearrangement of any of the ideas or thoughts or things of the time and space realm. It cannot be.

We've had enough of that already. Haven't we?

*

The change is a change of consciousness. A stepping back up to Truth!

And it happens when it's ready to happen. When we're ready.

And this is easy and difficult (Ha! We're still in duality... but things aren't as cut and dry as before). We start to embrace the paradox...

That we are tired and have fallen, but that we need to step up and the falling is a part of that (a 'prior condition')...

That we can be in time and space, where certain rules operate... but we are also of a Spiritual Essence where other rules operate and where things can be true simultaneously... because we're moving back to a consciousness of the Source... The One... the 'other-worldly' (non-worldly!) Nondual 'Everything and Nothing'.

*

Rather than that delineation that is solid and clear in the world of structures, rules, conditions, limits, physicality, separation and matter... we are shedding limitations... we choose to shed limitations... to return to Wholeness. Boxes are broken, labels discarded. We may not know this is what's happening... but it is.

Self-Inquiry is how it is happening. There is an examining of what is real, and what is not. Of what makes you happy, and what doesn't. Of what is useful and what isn't. Of what is freeing and what is restricting. Of what is needed and what can be left behind. Indeed, there is a whole re-evaluation of Life.

This is the Shift in Consciousness.

This is all part of the Journey.

All part of the Journey of Love!
How does it happen?

Like I say, a crisis of meaning. We choose to step up... to make the necessary changes. We empower ourselves... with knowledge... less external now, and more internal. This is indicative of the shift in focus. Away from external separation and toward internal wholeness. (And beyond even this duality! Internal Wholeness). You don't need to be aware that this is so at first... but after a while you will be.

It is all happening naturally.

Relax.

Less contraction, less stress. This is more about opening now, receiving your Divinity, seeing Who You Are, rather than struggling as a separate part out there in the world. But the struggle is all part of it! You have to search before you can find. And you are searching...

This very movement is the stirring of the movement of consciousness back in. We seek to find. And there is nothing else to find but Truth. If we are looking as openly and honestly and clearly and discerningly as we can, we will find it. And it will find us. It will draw us in. Intelligence, yes. Awareness, certainly. Shedding the blinkers, we are expanding Awareness of 'Who We Are' beyond the separation. Life attracts Life.

Indeed it was thinking we were separate that kept us apart.

It is Realising we are Whole that brings us back together.

No-one can realise it for you. This is the Beauty. This is the Journey!

You are Consciousness experiencing Itself!

That- This!- is how unique and special and important your Life is. All of our lives are! And Life Is. Each one of us fulfilling an aspect of Consciousness... providing it with a particular view, or angle on Itself, a particular flavour or version of Itself- one possibility of many, creating all possibility in form (or the closest physical appropriation of that Truth) and coming back in again... where that Truth is re-established directly, as is- rather than by less-than-whole re-presentation, or proxy).

Oneness returns to Itself.

*

How does the return movement happen, again?

Disillusionment with the way things are.
Feeling things are not Life-affirming.
Feeling that there must be another way.

That there must be 'more' to Life.

These are all precursors to change...
and after so many superficial changes
(re-arranging surface impressions, fashions, fads, quick fixes),
the shift happens.

The change of focus, in direction, in trajectory...
It happens.

And so we start to come back in. Because we choose to.
Individually, as separate body minds we choose to...
And as a Whole.

FOR WE ARE CONSCIOUSNESS CHOOSING.

(And Ultimately, there is only One Consciousness! Veiled in

apparent separation, yes... in time and space sense world separate... but to Spiritual Perception, United, Whole and One).

*

We've had our experience. Time to go Home!
Perfect mirrors to this in life-
'Tea time!' Enough play!

And yet coming back in- coming Home- This is an experience too! (Just as much as 'going out' 'was'...)...

And perhaps the most exciting one.
Because connecting to your Truth,
you begin to live it, to offer it,
to fulfil your own Self.

This is the fulfilment of Consciousness! On its Return Journey.

We spiritualise the world like this! It just happens... because it must! We are determined to live Truly!

The Search for meaning, the Spiritual Path, and the Remembrance of our Truth naturally create (or are the result of! It's all one cause and effect...) this inward movement.

With the force of our Own Being. The Inner Impulse of Nature. The Urge of Life to fulfil Itself by Knowing Itself. The Original Impulse of the Source...

We begin to realise our Wholeness for ourselves. As we do so, we cease to offer or accept tokens of the separation (as primary value), and we start offering and accepting Wholeness. For we naturally offer from where we are at. This is how consciousness operates- what we give off is what we are! And what we get.

The giving and the receiving are One.

This is what we teach the world!

We live from the inside out, rather than the outside in. From Wholeness rather than separative lack.

We still respect separation- for we see it is the means to experience. But we no longer privilege it as the only way. Privileging it as 'the only way' would be a stance that comes with the constricted Awareness that we are now freeing up.

Boundaries are dissolving... and yet we are ever-surer of ourselves as we return to Truth, aligning ever-closer to our natural qualities of Peace, Love, Being-ness.

Remembrance is pulling us Home, elevating with a 'gravity' of Spirit.

Across all times and spaces, we are returning.

This is the return part of the Journey...

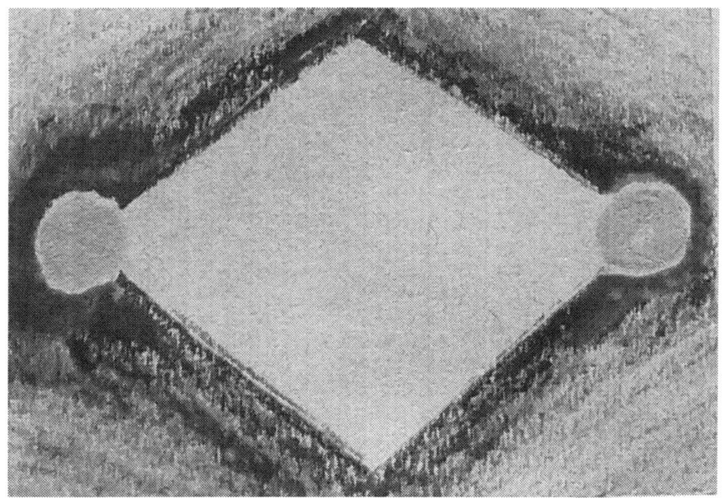

It's all the Natural Journey of Love. Of Self.

Consciousness's fragmentation and re-integration of/with Itself.

The expression of the Universe; of ourselves, reaches its limits (the crisis or Realisation point of the world and its people) and comes back in... To what is Real and True.

While natural for a time... the disconnect, the separation, is craziness if taken too far.

For the illusion no longer serves.

The Spirit That We Are.

It did for a time...
and for a space...

but Now we see its dissolution...

all our attachments, investments, holdings on let go...

we loosen our grip...

our grip has been loosened...

for there is nothing to hold onto but ourselves...

And We Are that already.

Always are, never cannot be.

And we see this.
We know this.

We Are,
We Are,
We Are.

*

No pre-conditions, no end terms, no need or want or must...

Life does not lie to us. We know what we need. Deep down, we know.

We re-establish ourselves in Truth by seeing our True Nature, and then it's plain sailing! (Well, er... there may be some challenges, some grand-finale epic final showdowns!).

But yes, your direction has been set, because you have set it. Your Consciousness attuned toward Deeper Meaning. And with that kind of ardent motivation, nothing can stand in your way.

For the conditions on Life have been removed, the contracts cleared... or are clearing... if nowhere else but in your own mind- your own Consciousness (for what and where else?! Yes, in the play we have 'other'- but only as dream-mirror to yourself).

And as the walls come down we Realise...

Boundless, Open, Free!

WE ARE IT!

This is Us.

Is you is me is This.

Yes, there are ups and downs... but we can ride them.

Because we see the context... we see the meaning... we see the Bigger Picture.

We see that we are (and always were!) Consciousness exploring, and not random meaningless selfish meat-mind units in a random mean and meaningless world.

Everything is infused with meaning and purpose,
for everything is seen as the Consciousness it is...
through nothing else but the Realisation of Its 'Is-ness'.

*

This is the Blessing, The Divine Blessing and Revelation of Life!

The folding back in.
The folding up of the playmat of experience.

The gathering back in of a duality that emerged from Oneness, and returns back into Oneness.

For the purpose of Play. A Divine Production of relative experience. Trials and tribulations... triumphs and adulations!

As we see both 'opposites' of any one spectrum, light-dark etc. … as the different ends of the same spectrum... the line is curled round and brought together into circle. The ends meet...

And We Are.

Embracing the duality as One.

*

We start(ed) with The Source.

And we end(ed) with The Source.

Divinely So.

This is the topsy-turvy, twinky-twonker mind-bender bit.

Our Journey is through time and space...

but started with Timelessness and ended with Timelessness.

The Timeless Source.

*

And what do we mean by Timelessness?

The absence of time.

*

Interesting. A Journey that 'started' with Timelessness and 'ended' with Timelessness.

How can we have a 'start' and an 'end' if there is no time? (How can we even have a journey?!).

*

And so this writing so far- bursting out and coming back in... has been presented as a linear 'Way of Seeing'. A linear Way of Seeing the experience of our Non-Linear, Timeless Source! ('Linear' being 'beginning' through to 'end'... like the progression of a line from 'time past' to 'time future'...).

A linear illustration of a Non-Linear Reality! (Non-linear because there are no 'two points' to draw a line between! Not Ultimately).

We have been indulging in the dream, for the sake of an exploration... and an explanation.

And now we have it.

*

Timeless Oneness has no two points! It is Timeless Oneness!

It's all happening Now! Here and Now! Because without time and space, here and now is all we have!

Pure Presence. The One. The Source.

Our Self.

*

Since Timelessness is the absence of time, Timelessness is Always HereNow. It must Be. Outside of time.

The same could be said of Oneness... One without a second. No two points of space. The absence of separate spatial reference points. Oneness is outside of space. Oneness at the 'beginning' and Oneness at the 'end' is Just Oneness! So it must be Here. For this is where existence is. Existence Is!

Timelessness is Oneness, and Oneness is Timelessness.

Source is Source is Source.

This is Pure Spirit Source Self. Independent of the time-space construct.

Here and Now. For in Timelessness... in Oneness... Where else? It is everywhere and nowhere. Now(-)here.

So anywhere 'we are' in the apparent world of time and space, we can be present to Timelessness. There is this possibility to 'tune in' to Timeless-Spacelessness... or 'tune out' of time-space... whichever way you look at it. To Be Where We Really Are.

Timeless Eternity (...not time that stretches on forever, but time's absence...), Source, God, One...

Is The Present Moment.

This Present Moment!

*

Only time and space say(s) otherwise.
Only time and space make(s) it appear otherwise.
The grid-like overlay, the bursting, spreading out and compartmentalisation... and our investment in it- in specific parts of it and not other parts.

Only minds that are locked in time and space keep consciousness at that level and knowingly or unknowing are complicit in the perpetuation of dream at expense of Reality.

And we have seen by now that the dream is not where we Primarily Are. Not where Love Ultimately Is, and not where world-problem solutions are to be found. Time and space are not our 'final resting place'... but a means through which experience is enabled, and had. Always, a 'getting there'.

Time and space are the same. They are the functions of the separation. The experience. Two objects far apart in space are far apart in time... for it takes time to get from one to another. We journey through space in time, just like we journey through time in space. All One Consciousness Journeying!

Time and space are the lines/grid/spectrum of combinations of possibility. The 'places' where Consciousness- otherwise Pure and 'set apart' ('on High')- can 'place' itself. Where it can exist beyond Timeless Spaceless Non-Existence/ Pure Existence. Where it can exist in experience... as we have seen.

The Present Moment is Pure Potential Spirit Essence.

At once independent of the world of experience...

...and yet the lifeblood of it. Consciousness! God!

The True Animating Force! That which makes everything happen.

*

Connected to (or established in) this Animating Force, time and space are Divine! They are Spiritualised. Returned to meaning and purpose. Not explicit single-minded purpose- but broad resting place of Awareness that infuses everything with the Divine Life-Energy of Love. Consciousness = God = Essence = Awareness = Love = Presence Here and Now.

And it is 'time and space' where this Presence can be felt. Well, 'outside' it... but the launch point- the springboard- into Timelessness is at any point within the time-space world. (And, like this, the 'time-space world' is, Truly Speaking, This!). You can 'tune in' to Timeless Spaceless Essence wherever you are in time and space. Wherever you find yourself!

It is in this time-space world that we have the opportunity to turn to Presence. Wherever we are in/on the time-space journey, the time-space map... we can stop and be present. And in those moments- in that Moment- This Moment- time and space are no longer time and space (no longer an object), but Timelessness. Spacelessness. Or 'Pure Space No-thingness'. It is beyond words.

A Divine Integration of Self.

*

We come to the Hub of the Wheel... bridging Spirit and Earth, Essence and experience.

And yet we can't privilege only the Essence at the expense of the experience... for they complement each other in the natural rhythm of Life. The drum beat is silence, noise, silence, noise, silence, noise, silence, noise... Silence.

We can, however, see the time-space experience in its correct context as in service to the Essence... and each one of us in service to that Essence. And that's not any sacrifice... when we realise We Are It.

There is no surrender in True Spirituality but to Ourselves. On The Deepest Level. That is, Our Self. The death of limitation, to the Unlimited... and its play, which is no longer limited, but serves as the channels through which the Unlimited operates and seeks to reflect Itself (naturally does), or sees Itself embodied (naturally is).

*

We are simply aligning with ourselves.

Sometimes we become unaligned in our experience...

but only to align once more.

(Duality, journey, the experience!).

And what we ultimately seek alignment with-
We Are Always It.

So enjoy it.

The Whole mad, beautiful show.

The Consciousness We Are.

*

We see all this.
We come to see all This.
All That Is.

Timelessness at the 'beginning' and Timelessness at the 'end' is only Timelessness. Just Timelessness.

One Timeless Being HereNow!

And as you see this... As You See This...

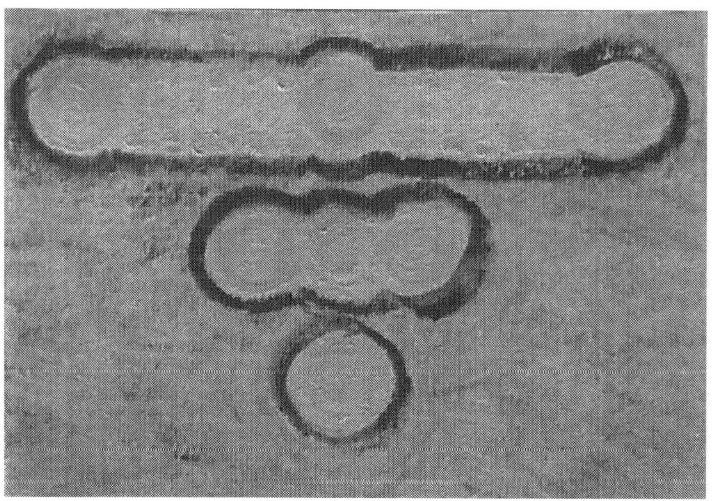

It all comes
back together...

...into The One it is, You Are.

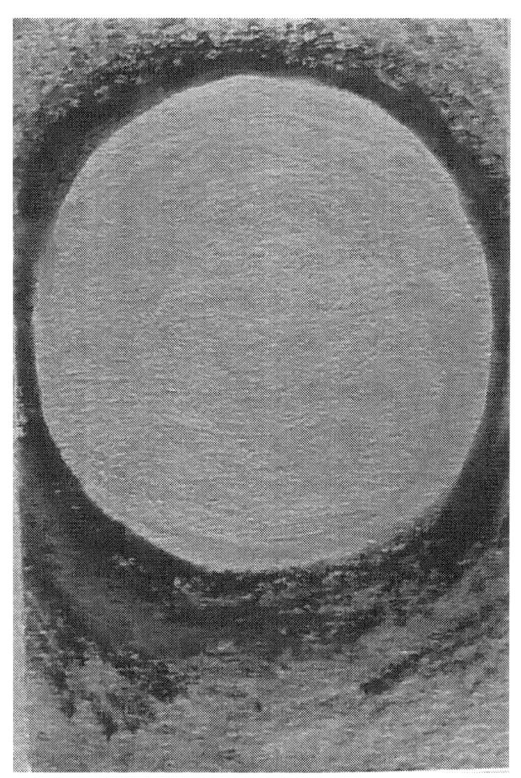

And you see
The Original
Light You Are.

Indeed, You Are...

This Original Light Seeing.

We All Are.

For the First Time (the last time... the only time)...

Eternally...
Now.

*

In time and space world
we appear separate for the sake of the experience
of this- forgetting and remembering again.

This is Consciousness Experiencing Itself-

And We Are It!

Always,
HereNow,
One.

We exist in Timelessness (as Wholeness) and time (as apparently separate part).

Each is true, on its own terms.

Oneness is our True Nature.

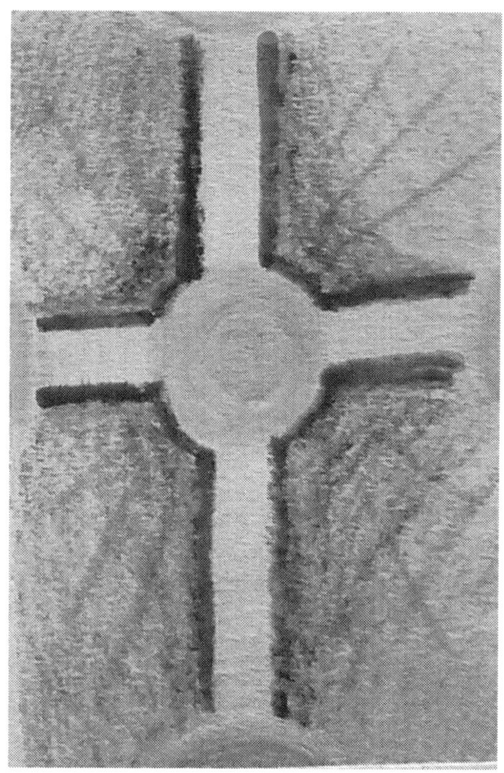

Timelessness/Wholeness/Consciousness/Love/Light
Pure Being: The Deeper Truth of Us.

We come to know this-
and live in the world
out of this Love we know we are. In it!

Here, having returned to our Source, we come out again in creation (across all times and spaces- personal, circumstantial, Universal...)... perhaps this 'time' experiencing with Remembrance. Perhaps never even 'leaving...'.

We could be returning Home in one respect, while creating in the world of 'separation' in another. But this time it is not separative, it is Whole... because the Being behind it is Whole. (And this is our experience... until awareness fades again...).

This Wholeness is not a false Unity of idea or its association...
It is a deep One of Direct Experience... depths...
deeply felt within
and naturally
brought out in whatever form in the world
feels right for you to honour it by- to honour yourself by.

To Be. Self-Sovereign Authority.

Not as homogenised
Non-Duality / Mindfulness drones...
but each as unique individuals
(of The One Unique Individual Oneness)
with unique talents
to offer in this world- and ourselves- and 'each other'-
from (and on) an innate
Spirit soul level.

*

You see... it's all about being True to Your Self- at whatever stage of the Journey you are at.

And you can't be anywhere else but where you are. And Where You Are.

It is when we try to be elsewhere that we lose perspective and get lost.

But there is no elsewhere...

...only Us...

And we Realise This...
Falling into a Greater Love with Ourself...

Free Fall...

Love.

*

The world is
Consciousness in motion.

We are the Whole
and we are this movement... this motion... Love...

Happening now... the Heart the intersection of Divine and worldly Being... all held together in One Great Spirit Love that allows it all to be. In Essence and experience...

Allow it all to be. And choose. What you want. For you are it Being!

Holding the worlds together...

The Centre of the Cross.

Heart of Stillness
Arms of Love and action
and feet to walk this Earth...
Diffusing Divinity with each step,
receiving Spirit on Earth and
elevating Earth to Spirit.

Immanence and Transcendence.

Nowhere else (to be)
but Here.

We are here to experience
and come back in

...and experience some more...

Out of and into and out of and into and in and out of and into ourselves.

Our Self.

One.

And many

And One...
and many...

And One.

Love Here Now.

We Are.

NathanGodolphin.com

Made in the USA
Lexington, KY
26 July 2017